CHARLES, BURROWS

&

CHARLES

SPECIAL THANKS

The author and publisher wish to give special thanks to Chris Connor at Charles/Burrows/Charles, whose assistance in putting this book together was absolutely invaluable.

Information in this book came from interviews the author conducted with all three partners as well as from promotional material provided by Charles/Burrows/Charles and articles from the University of Redlands alumni magazine, Channels, *and the* New York Post.

Published by Blackbirch Press, Inc.
One Bradley Road
Woodbridge, CT 06525

© 1995 Blackbirch Press, Inc.
First Edition

Printed in Canada

10 9 8 7 6 5 4 3 2 1

Library of Congress Cataloging-in-Publication Data

Greenberg, Keith Elliot.
    Charles, Burrows & Charles : TV's top producers / by Keith Elliot Greenberg. — 1st ed.
        p. cm. — (Partners II)
    Includes bibliographical references and index.
    ISBN 1-56711-136-X (lib. bdg.)
    1. Charles, Glen, 1943- —Juvenile literature. 2. Burrows, James, 1940- —Juvenile literature. 3. Charles, Les, 1948- —Juvenile litera-ture. 4. Television producers and directors—United States—Biography —Juvenile literature. 5. Television comedy writers—United States—Biography—Juvenile literature 6. Cheers (Television program)—Juvenile literature. [1. Charles, Glen, 1943-   . 2. Burrows, James, 1940-   . 3. Charles, Les, 1948-   . 4. Television producers and directors. 5. Television comedy writers. 6. Cheers (Television program)] I. Title. II. Title: Charles, Burrows, and Charles. III. Series
PN1992.4.A2G74 1995
791.45'0232'092273—dc20
[B]   94-44717
                                                                      CIP
                                                                       AC

P A R T N E R S

CHARLES, BURROWS

CHARLES

TV's Top Producers

Keith Elliot Greenberg

B L A C K B I R C H   P R E S S

W O O D B R I D G E ,   C O N N E C T I C U T

Table of Contents

Introduction: Where Everybody Knows Your Name   7

1. Glen and Les   13

2. Jim   27

3. Starting in TV   39

4. Mastering Television   50

5. Making Cheers   61

6. Creative Company   73

7. Highs and Lows   83

8. Closing Up   90

9. Moving Ahead   97

Appendix: Highlights from Eleven Years of Cheers   102

Glossary   106

Further Reading   107

Bibliography   107

Chronology   108

Index   110

The creative partnership of Glen Charles (left), James Burrows
(center), and Les Charles (right) has produced some of television's
most memorable and popular programs.

Where Everybody Knows Your Name

"When you have the right partners,

they just make your skills better."

—*Glen Charles*

It was a television show about a neighborhood bar, known not for its drinks or its food but for the people who came together there. Every week, millions of Americans tuned in to follow the soap-opera-like stories of Sam Malone, the former athlete who owned the place, and his colorful staff and customers. There was Sam's sometime love, Diane, an intellectual waitress more interested in art and literature than taking customers' orders; Cliff, a mailman by day and a know-it-all by night; and Norm, who was hiding from his wife, Vera.

No one can say what makes a television show a hit, but *Cheers*—the place "where everybody knows your name," as the theme song went—had all the right qualities. It was friendly and funny, and viewers cared enough about the characters to keep watching for eleven seasons.

Cheers was "kind of like a small town," says Ted Danson, the actor who played Sam. "When people see you and recognize *Cheers,* there's a warmth—an 'I've shared a lot of laughs with you' kind of nice feeling. I've seen the reflection of *Cheers* on people's faces."

By its final episode on May 20, 1993, *Cheers* had won 26 Emmy Awards—the highest honor in television—out of a record total of 111 nominations. One measure of the show's tremendous popularity is the dozens of *Cheers* bars that have opened across the United States, modeled after the welcoming place on the show.

"In our wildest dreams, we never thought that *Cheers* would be such a hit," says Les Charles, one of the three partners who created the show. "Our main goal was to do something we were proud of."

The partners' pride glistened throughout the series. Brothers Les and Glen Charles were writers who put their hearts into the program, creating situations on *Cheers* from events they had witnessed in their own lives. Director James Burrows—or Jim—came from a family involved in the Broadway stage. He saw each episode he directed as a little play.

Just like the bar in the program, the partnership of Charles, Burrows, Charles brought people together from different backgrounds. "I'm Jewish, they're Mormons," Jim says of his relationship with the Charles brothers. "They

A "family portrait" of some of the *Cheers* cast, taken on the set with members of the crew, Glen (front left), Heide Perlman with Jim (center) and Les in front, on the right.

come from a small town, I come from a big town. They're rural, I'm urban. They come from a non-show-business background, I come from a show-business background. They write, I direct. But somehow it all worked out. We always had this respect for one another."

For Jim, going into a partnership with two brothers was a challenge. Outsiders questioned whether the siblings would team up against him in disagreements. But Jim instead often found himself helping by being the third voice in the room.

"I felt like the third Charles brother," he says. "I understood their language. Because they have such a long history together, they share little expressions no one else understands. After awhile, they didn't have to stop and explain things to me. I knew exactly what they were talking about."

Says Glen, "The down side of partnership is you can never claim full credit for anything. In television, the writers, the actors, and the director all work together. But when you have the right partners, they just make your skills better."

He enjoys telling the story of the old Jewish man who could not get along with his associates, complaining, "Oy, partners!"

Then, Glen quickly adds with a smile, "I never had to say that."

"We always had this respect for one another."

As brothers, Les and Glen Charles share a special bond that strengthens their partnership.

Glen and Les

"If anybody would have told me

when we were growing up that I'd be

working with my brother one day,

I would have told him he was nuts."

—*Glen Charles*

Glen Charles never imagined that his baby brother would be his partner one day. "If anybody would have told me when we were growing up that I'd be working with my brother one day, I would have told him he was nuts," Glen says.

Glen was born on February 18, 1943, just outside Las Vegas, Nevada. Both of his parents were members of the Mormon faith. His father, Gerald, originally worked in a bank, but after several years in Las Vegas, he found a job in one of the city's numerous casinos. Glen's mother, Evelyn, was a teacher.

Gerald was raised in Utah, and Evelyn came from Idaho. They first traveled to Las Vegas on their honeymoon. Compared to the places they had lived, the city was electrifying: Stores and casinos were open all night and there was always lots of activity, no matter what time of day. In the casinos, roulette wheels spun, and slot machines rang. Tourists could spend all night going from ballroom to ballroom, watching the top entertainers in the country perform.

The highlight of the Charles' vacation was dancing past movie star Ava Gardner during a night out. "For these two people from rural backgrounds, to be dancing next to Ava Gardner was very exciting," Glen explains.

Gerald and Evelyn loved the glamorous town and decided to settle there. Les would later remember growing up in a home filled with happiness. "My parents had a successful marriage," he says, "and that always helps children later on in their own partnerships. If you've seen your parents get along, it's easy to get along with other people."

Les was born on March 25, 1948, Gerald and Evelyn's second and last child. Glen, five years old at the time, was confused by the new addition to the household. "I remember when Les came home from the hospital," he says. "I just looked at him, not sure what he was. Here was this little blob. I didn't know what to think of him."

In some ways, Les believes he had a typical writer's childhood. "If you go back and look at what most comedy writers were like growing up, you usually find a kid who's a little bit different," he explains, "a little goofy, an oddball in some way. If he wasn't the class clown, he may have been the class freak or geek. Those kinds of kids shouldn't feel bad about being different."

What made the Charles brothers different from many others was their religion. The Mormons have been a mystery to those people who did not understand their beliefs or their history. Those misunderstandings often led to outbreaks of violence in the past. In the nineteenth century, Mormons were frequently attacked. Joseph Smith, the group's founder, was killed by an angry mob in 1844.

"We grew up with the feeling of being outsiders," Les says. "Mormons were looked down upon as weird. We knew what it felt like to be part of a minority."

For young Glen and Les, even the Mormon lifestyle would occasionally lend itself to comedy. Children of all religions frequently find themselves joking around—instead of paying attention—in church. With no professional clergy, the Mormons rely on different members of the congregation to give the sermons. Because they are not used to addressing an audience, the lecturers sometimes made nervous mistakes. When this occurred, Glen and Les would giggle at the speakers.

"The people would say funny things without meaning it," Les now remembers. "They were good-hearted people, but it was easy to start laughing."

As happy as their childhoods were, the brothers were not always united. "We did not get along famously when we were growing up," Glen admits. When their parents went out, Glen would have to baby-sit his younger brother. Les would invite his friends over, and the boys would refuse to listen to Glen's orders. In reaction, Glen would become even more strict.

Other times, Les would try to tag along when Glen was with his friends. "I guess he thought I was a bit of a pest," Les admits now. "I was five years younger and wanted to hang out with the older guys. And he didn't want me around."

From time to time, Glen would play tricks on his sibling. "One time, he got a bow and arrow for Christmas or his birthday," Les recalls. "He took me out in the backyard. He gave me a cardboard box and told me to sit down on it. Then, he said I was the settler in the wagon train and he was the Indian. And he started shooting arrows at me. I still have a scar on my hand."

When Evelyn Charles noticed her children clashing, she would try to step in and referee. "They didn't always see eye to eye," she remembers. "But I taught them that, if you're smart, you solve your differences and work together."

Of course, most of the time, the boys got along. Les always secretly admired his older brother. "I idolized him," he says. "I thought he was great."

On one occasion, the brothers teamed up to sell lemonade in their neighborhood. Conditions were perfect for business—a hot, summer day in the Nevada desert. "We brought the lemonade out," Glen says. "I remember Les or I or the both of us took a drink of the lemonade to test it. One of the neighborhood kids saw and thought that was a violation of the health code! Whenever anybody would come by, the kid would say, 'Don't buy it. They already drank out of the pitcher.' I don't think we sold too much."

Like most American children growing up in the 1950s, the Charles brothers watched a great deal of television. They were especially fond of *The Honeymooners*, starring Jackie Gleason as Ralph Kramden, a Brooklyn bus driver who was always trying to find an easy road to fame.

"Every week, he would have a plan," Glen says. "He was going to get rich. He was going to move up at the bus company. You knew it was doomed to failure. But he always bounced back the next week with another idea. It was inspiring in a way—and it was very funny."

Another program the two brothers enjoyed was *The Dick Van Dyke Show*. Van Dyke played a comedy writer married to Mary Tyler Moore. Little did the boys realize that they would one day be comedy writers themselves—and later would even work for Mary Tyler Moore's show.

"Shows about writers don't tend to be funny," Glen says. "But something about this

Evelyn Charles said of her sons, "I taught them that, if you're smart, you solve your differences and work together."

show was. You saw Dick Van Dyke at work, then
he went home and he had a pretty normal life.
The average person could relate to him. Even
though he had a different kind of job, he ran
into the same problems as everybody else."

On most Saturday afternoons, the boys
would get out of the house and would go to the
movies—screaming at horror films and laughing
at comedies featuring Laurel and Hardy and the
Three Stooges.

During a summer vacation in Arizona, the
brothers amused their father with a puppet
show. "We had these little hand puppets," Glen
says. "And we had a little stage. I think it's the
first time we ever worked together to entertain
someone." Back home in Nevada, Glen added
to his presentation. "Glen had a lot of puppets,"
Les recalls. "He had puppets and marionettes
and even a couple of dummies. We'd do shows
for each other and the neighborhood kids. But
we never sold tickets. I wonder why we didn't
have the brains to do that."

As early as third grade, Les knew what he
wanted to do as an adult—he was going to be a
writer. Every week, he would write a new chapter of an ongoing adventure story. Then, after
recess at his school, he would read the latest
episode to the class.

Once the boys got older, they realized one of
the reasons why their parents had settled in Las
Vegas. Every great comedian in America passed

through the city and performed at its casinos. Glen and Les could not resist seeing people such as Don Rickles, Shecky Green, and other big comedy stars. "We were underage," Les says, "so we had to stand way in the back so no one would see us. But we'd get caught a lot."

As a result of laughing at the same jokes, "we developed very similar senses of humor," Les says. "And that helped us later on when we were writing for television. At least we agreed on what was funny and what wasn't."

A young Les and Glen, ages eight and thirteen respectively, pose for a photo while out for dinner with father Gerald and mother Evelyn.

Glen attended Basic High School, which was constructed to educate the children of the many workers at a nearby chemical factory called Basic Magnesium. He played football on Basic's team, participated in student government, and was once asked to judge a special competition involving junior high school students.

It was a writing contest, and Les took first prize. "I don't know if Glen pulled any strings," Les laughs. "He probably voted against me."

When Les entered Basic High, he also involved himself in civic activities and sports. "When I was a sophomore, our football team lost every game," he says. "I remember the team that became the state champions beat us 75-0. On the last touchdown, the runner knocked me down and ran right over me. You might say it was only a football game, but I think that experience permanently scarred every member of the team. When we'd see kids from other schools, we'd turn our letter sweaters inside out."

By now, Glen had left Las Vegas to attend the University of Redlands in Redlands, California—about seventy miles east of Los Angeles. The state of California had the same glamorous appeal for him that Las Vegas had had for his parents. "Southern California meant the movie business, the ocean, the beautiful women," he says.

At Redlands, Glen studied literature, speech, and drama. For the first time, he acted—and learned what it felt like to perform for a crowd

and listen to instructions from a director. He was
also the master of ceremonies and wrote routines
for the talent show. During visits home, Glen
would often talk to his younger brother about
books. The older sibling favored Ernest
Hemingway, Irwin Shaw, and Joseph Heller,
among other authors.

After graduation, Glen attended law school at
the University of California at Berkeley. "I didn't
exactly know what I wanted to do," he says. "A
lot of my friends were going to law school. So I
took the law school entrance exam. When I
passed, I decided to go."

After the first year, though, Glen decided he
did not want to be a lawyer. Although he had
done well in his law studies, he now enrolled in
graduate school at San Francisco State University. There, he received a master's degree in
1968 in language arts—combining literature,
philosophy, and other studies.

"I really, to be frank, was kind of aimless,"
he says. "I didn't know what kind of career I
wanted."

Les followed Glen to the University of
Redlands—after first attending the University of
Nevada at Reno and the University of Nevada at
Las Vegas. The younger Charles brother studied
English and film and reviewed movies for the
Bulldog student newspaper.

At one point, Les visited his older brother in
San Francisco, and the two quickly got into a

discussion about the movies they liked: *The Graduate*, the story of a young man who does not know what to do with his life after college; *Bonnie and Clyde*, about the famous gangster couple; and the futuristic *2001: A Space Odyssey*. The little fights of their childhood had, by now, been forgotten; the brothers realized they had so much in common.

"It was the first time we talked to each other as adults," Glen remembers.

Les's college years would affect the rest of his life. While working as a bartender at the Gay '90s Pizza Parlor in Redlands, he met the man who would later become the inspiration for the character Norm on *Cheers*. He also met his wife Zora.

"I've known her for twenty-four years, and we've been married for twenty-three," he says. "She's been with me through the good times, through the lean times, through all of this."

Following his 1971 graduation, Les worked briefly as a gardener. Then, he and Zora became teachers.

Les hated his job as a substitute teacher at a tough junior high school in Pomona, California. "It was a hideous nightmare," he says. "A lot of the kids were angry at the world. I didn't feel like a teacher, I felt like a cop—and a victim. I couldn't loosen up because that's a weakness. So I'd just have to be mean all day. Boy, that gets to be a drag."

The little fights of their childhood had, by now, been forgotten; the brothers realized they had so much in common.

Glen was working at a Los Angeles advertising agency as a copywriter. His tasks included writing ads—or "copy"—for fishing tackle, hiking gear, and other sporting goods. Although he found the assignments easy, he longed to do something more creative. But while there, he also learned how to take criticism of his writing—a skill he would find useful once he began working in television. "When my first few scripts were rejected, it didn't bother me," he says. "I was used to having my writing criticized, and I knew it didn't reflect on me as an individual. Les didn't have the same background, so I think it was harder for him."

Both brothers agreed they wanted to change careers. The problem was they did not know what their new jobs should be. One afternoon, the two went to a movie together. Afterwards, instead of going home, they had a long conversation. "We found ourselves talking about how unhappy we were with our lives," Glen says. "At the same time, we talked about television shows we liked—*The Mary Tyler Moore Show, All in the Family, M*A*S*H.* So we decided—since we both had writing backgrounds—that we should start writing for television."

For the next couple of months, the brothers struggled. With so many people in southern California trying to become writers—and so few scripts actually making it onto the television screen—friends wondered if the two were lost in some type of dream. But the pair believed that their partnership would be successful.

"We believed in us," says Les. "We didn't get encouragement from anybody outside our family. So we kept each other's spirits high. When one felt dejected, the other would be encouraging. We were lucky that we never hit the dumps at the same time."

This kind of brotherly support kept both Glen and Les focused on their goals for the future. Fortunately for them, that future would soon start to take shape in many exciting ways.

Jim Burrows came to television with a lifetime's experience in show business.

Chapter 2

Jim

"I didn't want to be in show business."

—*Jim Burrows*

Entertainment was James Burrows's family business. His talented father, Abe Burrows, was a well-respected writer and producer, known by everyone in the theater.

Abe Burrows first showcased his writing skills in the 1930s, when families gathered around the radio every night to listen to programs. He wrote comedy routines for comedians and, by 1941, was considered good enough to create the show *Duffy's Tavern*, which was broadcast on the CBS radio network.

By the end of the decade, he had his own radio program, *The Abe Burrows Show*. Listeners tuned in to hear Abe tell jokes, play the piano, and sing the humorous songs he composed.

In 1950, Abe made a huge impact on the entertainment field when he co-authored *Guys and Dolls*, a play about gamblers, con artists, and preachers. The hit show broke records on Broadway, making millions of dollars in over 1,200 performances. It remains one of the most celebrated plays in the history of the American theater, and has been revived over the years.

In 1961, working with composer Frank Loesser, Burrows wrote and directed *How To Succeed In Business Without Really Trying*, the story of a window washer who rises to become a top executive. The show was so well-liked that Burrows won a Pulitzer Prize, the greatest honor a writer can receive for his or her work.

Among Abe's other notable scripts: *Can Can* in 1953, *What Makes Sammy Run* in 1964, and *Cactus Flower* in 1965.

Additionally, he directed *Two On the Aisle*, *Reclining Figure*, *Breakfast at Tiffany's*, *Forty Carats*, and *Four on a Garden*.

In 1956, he wrote the movie *The Solid Gold Cadillac* and, in 1979, authored his autobiography *Honest Abe: Is There Really No Business Like Show Business?*

James, called "Jim" or "Jimmy" by his friends, was born to Abe and Ruth Burrows in Los Angeles on December 30, 1940. There was only one other child in the family, a sister, who today, as Laurie Burrows Grad, writes cookbooks and does cooking demonstrations on television.

When Jim was five, his parents separated. The boy moved to New York City with his mother,

Jim, age twelve.

growing up in the well-to-do Upper West Side neighborhood of Manhattan. Several years later, Abe Burrows would also move to New York and become close to his son.

As a youngster, Jim spent a lot of time in his father's apartment, listening to playwrights and authors telling tales of the stage. "As a kid, I didn't think it was strange to be around celebrities," Jim says. "The theater was what my father did for a living. It was like my father was a tailor, and I took over the shop when he retired. Doing what I do now is like a tailor's son who learns to make a good suit."

Many afternoons, Jim says, he was "dragged to a lot of my father's rehearsals. I was dragged to a lot of his TV shows. Being that my father didn't live with us and he was so busy, we were around show business all the time. When he wanted to see us, and he had something else to do that day, he took us along."

Life in the theater did not always feel glamorous. Like any child brought to his father's workplace, Jim occasionally felt bored. "When you're a kid, you're in tow. You go wherever your parents take you. I didn't feel the special nature of where I was until I got older."

In the 1950s, Abe Burrows was a regular face on television. On a program called *PM East, PM West*, he would trade jokes and stories with the host, Mike Wallace. Wallace was an actor who had starred in *Reclining Figure*, a show Abe had directed a few years earlier. Later, he would become known all over the world as a legendary investigative TV journalist and host of the very popular news show *60 Minutes*.

One time, Jim was on the set when a new performer was introduced: a young singer from Brooklyn named Barbra Streisand. Back then, nobody realized that she was destined to become a very famous personality who would sing for presidents and star in movies. "But she was great," Jim recalls, "and you knew it."

Jim was also impressed with performers he observed from a distance. At home, he'd amuse himself by watching comedian Phil Silvers play Sergeant Bilko in the television show *You'll Never Get Rich.* Silvers played an army sergeant who preferred coming up with schemes to working hard. The soldiers in Bilko's unit would often be drawn into the scams. Jim remembers jokes flowing from the comedian's mouth "at a rapid fire pace." To the boy, the Bilko character was a lot like Fagan, leader of a gang of thieves in the Charles Dickens classic, *Oliver Twist.*

"He was a hustler," Jim says. "But he made you love him."

The youngster was also a fan of *Car 54, Where Are You?*, a comedy about a group of goofy New York City cops. "They had the same writers as Bilko," Jim says. "And the show was just as funny."

Then, there was Lucille Ball, who starred with her husband, Desi Arnaz, in *I Love Lucy.* Desi played a band leader at a popular club. His wife—never happy with her role sitting at home—was constantly coming up with strate-gies to sneak into his shows. Frequently, she tried to lure her landlords, cranky Fred Murtz and his wife Ethel—played by William Frawley and Vivian Vance—into the plots.

Lucille Ball "did comedy better than any-body," Jim says. "She was a wonderful physical comedian." He noted that she could crack up an audience by twisting her mouth or cocking her head a certain way. At times, Lucy would react to another actor by making a funny noise. On other occasions, she'd draw out a joke, building up viewers' expectations until they nearly exploded over the punchline.

"She'd milk the audience," Jim explains, "leading them along. Finally, they'd just roar with laughter."

Jim wasn't sure that he wanted a career in entertainment. "Through college," he recalls, "I didn't want to be in my father's business at all. I didn't want to be in show business."

Yet, despite his objections, Jim could not stay away from the stage. He auditioned to become a member of the Metropolitan Boys Chorus, a group consisting of the most talented youngsters in New York City.

"They'd come to your school and ask you to sing, 'My Country Tis of Thee,'" Jim explains. "If you were good, you got to perform with all these opera singers. For five years, I was on stage, getting three dollars a performance."

And he attended Music and Art High School, one of several public schools in New York City open to young actors and artists. Because he loved to sing, Jim took special courses to better his voice.

By this time, the radio was filled with the sounds of New York kids like "Dion and the Belmonts" from the Bronx and "Frankie Lymon

"I rebelled during my first year [at Yale drama school], then I said, 'This is something I want to do'."

Young Jim visits the front of the Metropolitan Opera in New York City with his father, Abe Burrows.

and the Teenagers" from Manhattan. All of these youngsters had started out in their neighborhoods, singing harmony on street corners.

"It was a lot of fun to be at Music and Art," Jim says. "It was very exciting. Everybody was singing in the streets."

"The Music and Art students were all from different ethnic and economic backgrounds. But they were drawn together by their love of entertainment. Before and after school, they'd stand on the corner belting out 'Why Do Fools Fall in Love?,' 'Book of Love,' and other tunes with that same doo-wop sound."

But Jim still clashed with his father on the subject of college. Abe wanted his son to study the theater, but Jim chose instead to major in government affairs at Oberlin College in Ohio. Although his college courses didn't really interest him at all—he found government affairs quite boring—young Jim was not ready to admit that fact to his father.

He did, however, give in a bit to the tug he felt toward the theater. Between his sophomore and junior years in college, Jim took a job in a summer stock theater group that performed plays in Virginia. He helped to build sets and hang lights, working mostly behind the scenes on the many different technical aspects of production. "I liked it, but I was still fighting it," Jim admits today.

After graduation, the gifted young man was accepted into the elite Yale School of Drama. To most aspiring actors, this would have been the opportunity of a lifetime. But Jim was less than enthusiastic. "I went to the Yale School of Drama at my father's demand," he says.

Then, something changed. After acting in plays and socializing with students who loved music and drama, Jim developed a different attitude. "I rebelled during my first year," he says. "Then I said, 'This is something I want to do.'"

Jim tried his hand at writing plays. "I was terrible," he says. "I was not a writer."

But Jim also began directing. He remembers supervising a scene from the play *The Cherry Orchard*, as well as one from his father's prize-winning *Guys and Dolls*.

"It was great," Jim recalls. After battling his father's wishes for so many years, he realized that his famous father had been right about the theater all along. It really was the right place for Jim to be.

After graduating from Yale in 1965, Jim was happy to get a job with his father. He worked backstage as an assistant stage manager on plays like *Breakfast at Tiffany's* and *Forty Carats*. Whenever an actor or actress would have a suggestion, Abe would always halt his busy schedule to listen to it. At the same time, the producer would hear out his son's ideas about changing a scene or a joke in a play.

"He would never discourage me," Jim says. "He would always say, 'That's interesting' or 'Maybe.' Or he'd give a reason why something wouldn't work. I was never put down or made to feel embarrassed for making any comments."

It was a philosophy that Jim would later bring to the set of *Cheers*, where the cast and partners were always encouraged to openly speak their minds.

"My father believed that you may know a lot more than a lot of people," Jim explains, "but someone might make some small suggestion that will start your mind going. And that's how I function now. It's always decision by committee, a blending of other people's ideas."

Today, Jim uses many of his father's directing techniques. "When he didn't want an actor to overreact to a joke, he'd try to get him or her to be more thoughtful," Jim explains. "He'd say, 'Think of the top of your head as having three holes in it. And you have three three balls up there, too. And you're trying to roll a ball into each hole. He was trying to get the actor to concentrate—to really think about the joke. Instead of taking the obvious approach—roaring out loud—maybe the best response was chuckling slightly, the way a person would act naturally."

When an actor would follow another one around on stage, Abe would advise them to think about pigeons. "Have you ever seen pigeons walk?" Jim explains. "One follows closely behind the other, bobbing and mimicking. It's a way of following a person affectionately."

Sometimes, Abe would look away from the action on stage, and would focus more on how a scene "felt." Jim remembers that "He'd go backstage and listen to the rhythm of a scene, rather than relying on images. He hated to be backstage and to not hear anything coming from the actors—he felt someone should always be talking or doing something. When he wouldn't hear dialogue, he'd say, 'There's a silence. And I know that no one's out there dancing, so I'm in trouble.'"

When he's on the set, Jim will occasionally try some of his father's old directing techniques. While he doesn't walk out of view of the actors, he will sometimes put his head down, looking away, and will try to "hear the beat."

Despite all his schooling, Jim feels that his best theatrical education came from watching his father and other masters at their craft.

"You can't learn to direct in a classroom," Jim explains. "You have to rely on experience, instinct, and talking to the actors. And through trying out different things, you slowly learn what an audience thinks is funny."

Starting in TV

"The first break was more exciting

than anything that came afterwards."

—*Les Charles*

During the early 1970s, the Charles brothers decided to write scripts for their favorite TV shows "on spec." That's a term—taken from the phrase "on speculation"—used to describe sending out scripts "cold," with no previous contact or request for material. No studio even knew that the Charles brothers existed. The brothers would simply write what they considered a good script, drop a copy of it in the mail, and hope it would catch the eye of a television executive somewhere. Under the best circumstances, the brothers hoped to have their script purchased, which might lead to a job offer. Under the worst circumstances, no one would bother reading what they sent.

"Nobody asked you to do it," Glen explains. "You weren't sure if you would get paid for it. But it was a sample of your work to show."

The two were told that no one in Hollywood read a script unless an agent presented it. Since they did not know any agents, they opened the phone book and looked for one. The first couple of agents Glen and Les called were not interested in them. They preferred to have clients who had already had scripts produced, rather than a teacher and an ad writer who were trying to break into the television business.

After an endless series of phone calls, one man was finally willing to work with the pair. Looking back, Glen says, "It's probably because he was desperate for clients."

The one program both brothers loved was *The Mary Tyler Moore Show.* The two watched the comedy every week and were familiar with all the characters. They decided to tailor their first script for that show, and the agent sent it out. They heard nothing for a long time afterwards.

Because they did not want to be idle, Glen and Les started writing for other programs. "We decided to watch every show we liked and write a script for each of them," Glen says.

After those shows rejected the young writers also, they came up with another strategy. "We said, 'Let's start writing for shows we *don't* like,'" Glen remembers. "'We have to get in somehow.'"

The two wrote for comedy programs, detective shows, even westerns. Either they were told

"We were living out of a Volkswagen bus," Les remembers, "... and, frankly, it was one of the happiest periods of our lives."

that their material was not quite "right for the program," or they heard nothing at all.

Meanwhile, Les and his wife Zora quit their teaching jobs, convinced that the brothers would soon get their big break. "We were living out of a Volkswagen bus," Les says. "We just went from campground to campground. We had all our possessions in that bus and, frankly, it was one of the happiest periods of our lives. Everything was so simple. Everything we owned was right in that one vehicle. We had a lot of faith—I don't know where we got it. And Zora gave me a lot of encouragement."

Thousands of people try to change their careers and start over as writers or actors. Only a very small percentage realize their dreams, but Glen and Les were lucky. After seven months of sending scripts everywhere, they received a call from *M*A*S*H*, a comedy about a medical team tending to American soldiers during the Korean War in the 1950s.

Actually, the producers of *M*A*S*H* were not interested in using the script the Charles brothers had sent. There were more exterior—or outside—scenes than they wanted. But they could tell that Glen and Les were good writers and wanted to work with them.

To this day, Les believes that experience "was the high point of our careers. The first break was more exciting than anything that came afterwards."

After a long discussion with the producers of
*M*A*S*H*, the brothers put together a script
that made them proud. Everyone at the program
seemed to like it, too. The days of begging for
work seemed to be over. An original script, written by Glen and Les, was finally going to be on
television.

When their episode aired, the two had a
party for their friends. Everyone watched the
show, cheering loudly when the brothers' names
appeared in the closing credits.

"We thought we had it made," Glen says.
"So I quit my job, too."

Then, the unexpected happened. For a number of months, they did not sell anything else.

"We went three or four months thinking that
was it," Les says, "that we'd sold this one script,
and we'd never sell another script again. That
was probably the most depressing period of our
careers."

Worse yet, neither brother was working, and
the bills were piling up. Although they knew
that top television writers drove sports cars and
lived in mansions, Glen and Les were not making that kind of money. They did not even have
a means of supporting themselves.

"We were paid well for the *M*A*S*H*
script," Glen remembers now. "But when you
divided the money by two and had to make it
last for who knows how long, it wasn't really all
that much."

In the midst of their misery, they received a pleasant surprise. The first script they had ever sent out had finally been read by the people at *The Mary Tyler Moore Show*. It had taken the producers ten months to find their work among the huge assortment of mail they received. But the Charles brothers' writing caught their interest. Now, *The Mary Tyler Moore Show* also wanted the two to come in for a meeting.

In addition to working as an actress and the star of her program, Mary Tyler Moore and Grant Tinker, her husband at the time, had a production company—called MTM— that was responsible for some of the most exciting programs on television. Aside from *The Mary Tyler Moore Show*, they produced *Phyllis, The Bob Newhart Show, Rhoda, The Betty White Show,* and *The Tony Randall Show*. Later, they would switch from comedies to dramas, producing the award-winning police program, *Hill Street Blues*. The critics loved Mary Tyler Moore's productions. Writers and actors everywhere wanted to work for the company.

Now MTM was offering Glen and Les each a job—less than a year after they had made the decision to write for television.

"It turned out all the extra writing we did was a waste of time," Les jokes. "The first script we ever sent out was to *The Mary Tyler Moore Show*. It took them about a year to get back to us, but then they wanted to hire us. So I guess all those other scripts didn't mean a lot in the way things turned out."

Their first assignment was rewriting several episodes of *Phyllis*, which starred the comedic actress Chloris Leachman. These were scripts crafted by other writers that, somehow, did not work: Either the scenes were too long, the plots did not make sense, or the jokes were not funny. It was up to Glen and Les to change the scripts around—by adding new lines, creating different characters, and coming up with gags to make the audience laugh.

The other staff members at *Phyllis* could tell how anxious Glen and Les were to make a good impression. "We were the new kids," Les says. "We were struggling to prove ourselves."

On the first day, the Charles brothers' bosses told them something that was guaranteed to make the pair work hard—and work scared. Les recalls, "They brought us in and they said, 'You have to do a rewrite. We're going to try you out for a day. If we're not happy with what you do after today, you don't have a job anymore.' I'm still not sure if they meant it, or if they were just kidding around with us. But you couldn't believe the pressure we felt. Think about it—to have one day to sink or swim."

The first day worked out fine, as did the next day, and the day after that. Soon, Glen and Les graduated from doing rewrites to coming up with new scripts themselves.

"When we wrote, we always tried to *hear* the voices of the characters we were writing about," Glen says. "There are some very good joke writers out there. These are funny people, but they can't make the jokes come out of a certain character's mouth. And that's a big problem in television. A funny joke that you tell at a party, with a punchline, is not necessarily what a character might say on a TV show or in a movie."

Fortunately for Glen and Les, they did not have this flaw. The other people in the MTM offices liked the way the characters sounded in the brothers' scripts. With each successful episode, the pairs' confidence grew.

"We couldn't have been happier," Glen says. We had steady employment and were very satisfied professionally. We couldn't believe we were working as comedy writers."

While the two were writing for *Phyllis*, they met James Burrows, who had been brought in to direct several episodes. He had first met Mary Tyler Moore in 1965, when he was second assistant stage manager—one of the lowest backstage jobs—for the play, *Breakfast at Tiffany's*, on one of New York's Broadway stages. Mary was one of the stars.

Jim remembers, "I would run around getting Mary hamburgers from this place she liked called McGuinesses. And during breaks, I'd talk with her and her husband, Grant Tinker, and became kind of friendly with them."

Mary went on to become a television celebrity, and Jim continued working in the theater, eventually rising to the role of director. Because of the long hours, he was too busy to pay much attention to what was popular on television. One evening, though, while he was in the middle of working on a play in Wallingford, Connecticut, he turned on the television set and saw *The Mary Tyler Moore Show*.

"I watched it closely, and it was very good," he says. "Really, it was like a half-hour play. Since I was directing plays now, I thought I was good enough to start directing these little plays on television."

Jim was fairly confident Mary Tyler Moore would remember him. But he wanted to make sure he approached her in an appropriate and impressive way. People she had met everywhere were always calling on her for favors. Jim wanted Mary to know that he was not just another eager fan, but that he had something special to contribute to her program.

For three months, he wrote and rewrote a letter to the actress, trying to come up with the right phrases. "I wanted to write the perfect letter," he says, "something that would encourage her to get in touch with me to work on the show." Two weeks after he mailed the message, Jim received a phone call from Tinker. Both he and Mary had read the letter and wanted to work with Jim.

What first struck the Charles brothers about Jim was his ability to get everybody to like him—even the most difficult performers. Because the director is the person who tells the actors what to do, many directors make the mistake of offending the cast by being pushy or arrogant. There is a famous story in Hollywood about a director who had one of his decisions questioned by an actor.

"I don't understand why we should do things this way," the performer said.

"Because my house is bigger than yours," the director shot back cockily.

Jim's style of directing was quite different. Many of his co-workers believe that because he was sure of his skills, he felt no need to be boastful or quarrelsome.

"Of all Jim's talents, the most valuable one is he gets along with actors," Les observes.

Says Glen, "Certain people have to have their own way. Jimmy is not that way at all. You can reason with him. You can talk with him."

Jim remembers first meeting the Charles brothers in an office before a meeting about the show *Phyllis*. At first, he thought they were awfully quiet, but they soon made him smile. He found that, as the years went by, the two brothers became increasingly good at making their director friend laugh. As time passed, the three also grew closer as colleagues and felt they had a lot in common.

"We're similar people," Jim explains with a smile. I don't think you can say that any of us likes to entertain—none of us ever wanted to be actors in a show. But all three of us like to make people laugh."

To the Charles brothers, James Burrows was a welcome addition to the *Phyllis* set—the type of guy they could see themselves working with for a very long time.

Chapter 4

Mastering Television

"It's thrilling to see an audience laugh

at something you wrote

and it can be devastating

if they don't laugh."

—*Glen Charles*

James Burrows and the Charles brothers had finally arrived. All three had dreamed of working for television, and now they were actually doing it. But, in the highly competitive world of show business, one has to constantly improve. It is easy to go from being a star to a "has-been" in a very short time.

The three men were determined not to allow this to happen to them. They spoke with other professionals to gain tips and learn from their mistakes. They watched the actors closely, to better understand their craft. Most of all, they projected a positive attitude. Each of the three wanted to strengthen his talents and knowledge.

Many of the comedies on television today are performed in front of a live studio audience. If a performance is good, people laugh and applaud. If the show does not work, the crowd is quiet.

To many working in television comedy, hearing silence is worse than hearing boos.

"It's thrilling to see an audience laugh at something you wrote," Glen says. "And it can be devastating if they don't laugh."

At times, this catastrophe cannot be prevented. A writer may think that a certain scene is hysterically funny. When the director reads the script, he or she agrees. Then, the actors—swept up in the positive feelings on the set—become convinced that the audience will howl with laughter. Unfortunately, for some reason, sometimes no one laughs. It may be because they do not understand the jokes, or they simply may not find the material amusing.

One story popular in Hollywood involves a group of writers who came up with a joke about a man with a funny-sounding last name. Everyone else on the set thought the idea was foolproof, so the writers added several more jokes about the same name. On show night, however, the first time the man's name was mentioned, the audience did not react. Now, the writers knew they were in trouble. There were about a dozen similar jokes still to come—and probably all would get the same dull response as the first. The rest of the show seemed to go on forever, with each mention of the name falling flatter than the one before.

Most writers agree that the best way to make sure that something is really funny is to try it out on numerous people. Even if a routine does not work at first, there may be ways to make it come alive—if people are willing to work together to improve it.

"If you have a joke and it doesn't work, you have a number of choices," Jim says. "If you don't do anything about it, maybe the whole bit will be cut out of the show. But I try to come at the joke from a different angle—maybe if you say it with a funny hat on, it will work. It's important to keep the ball in the air. You try other things until you discover *why* the joke doesn't work. Then, you do something new to improve it."

Because jokes poke fun at people, there is always the risk of offending somebody when doing comedy. Humor is a good way to make people think about things, but if you make them angry, they may not want to watch the show any longer. This happened once, with a particular episode of *Phyllis*. On the program, the main character worked for a San Francisco city councilman. In one episode, Les created a gag about another city councilman who was a liar. He named the man Mendelson. "I don't know where I got the name from," he remembers. "Maybe I was listening to Mendelssohn, the German composer."

What Les did not realize was that there actually *was* a person named Mendelson who was a city councilman in San Francisco. The writer had

"If you have a joke and it doesn't work, you have a number of choices," Jim says. "…I try to come at the joke from a different angle."

not bothered to check on this, and neither had anyone else working for the show. When the program aired, the real Mendelson was furious. This was a politician who relied on the voters' trust. Now, because of one joke, he was worried that the people in San Francisco would think that he was a liar.

"The next week, we had to make a public apology on the air," Les says. Viewers were told that the Mendelson on the show was simply a writer's creation and that he and the real city councilman had nothing in common.

As a young writer, Les was worried that the mistake would ruin his career. "I was so scared," he says. "I thought I was going to get fired."

Luckily, the city councilman appeared to be satisfied with the apology, and nobody complained about the joke afterwards. Les was a good writer, and his bosses were happy with him. He and Glen continued working on *Phyllis* for a year and a half, until the show finally went off the air.

At that point, they went to *The Bob Newhart Show*, a popular program about a psychologist in Chicago. No longer just writers, the Charles brothers had now been promoted to producers. Their job still included writing scripts, however, as well as coming up with story ideas and supervising other writers.

Glen could not help laughing at his circumstances. "It was kind of interesting," he says.

"When we were sending out scripts to everybody, *The Bob Newhart Show* was one of the shows that rejected us."

After *The Bob Newhart Show* ended, the Charles brothers began working on *Taxi*, a comedy about a group of oddballs who were cab drivers in New York City. Since the brothers had only lived in Nevada and California, writing and producing for this show was a difficult task for them. They had to learn the way New Yorkers

Jim, Glen, and Les worked together on *Taxi* in their early days.

thought, spoke, and acted. The pair spent a lot of time in New York City, riding around in cabs and observing both drivers and customers. Plus, a friend of theirs from Brooklyn offered them advice on how a certain character might react to a specific situation.

Valuable information about New York also came from their old friend James Burrows. The New York-raised director had remained in the television business after *Phyllis* ended. When *Taxi* started, its creators decided that they wanted Jim Burrows to direct most of the episodes. Once again, the Charles brothers were united with their favorite director.

Glen and Les noticed that Jim had not changed. Although he was now one of the top directors in the television business, he was still the type of guy who made actors feel comfortable on the set. For his part, Jim felt that the writers had become even funnier with time.

Once, the director decided to catch up with some work while relaxing on a plane. He opened up one of the Charles brothers' *Taxi* scripts and was soon howling with laughter. "I roared," he says. "The stewardess had to come over and ask me if I was alright."

The cast of *Taxi* was one of the most gifted in the history of television. Stars like Marilu Henner, Judd Hirsch, Christopher Lloyd, Tony Danza, and Danny DeVito went on to have incredibly successful careers after the show ended.

The cast of
Taxi was one
of the most
gifted in the
history of
television.

But, of all the cast, the Charles brothers and Jim most remember Andy Kaufman, who played the foreign-born cab driver, Latka Gravas.

Kaufman lived by a different set of rules than the rest of the world. For example, the other cast members would sometimes complain that he was allowed to come to the set later than everyone else. Kaufman, it seems, had a disorder called "day/night reversal." He would wake up when most people were going to bed, stay up all night, and then sleep all day. Because of this problem, the producers allowed him to begin work after everyone else had finished lunch.

Recalls Glen, "Andy was unique, and we pretty much let him go in whatever direction he wanted. He was one of the strangest individuals I ever met."

"Andy was from a different planet," Les says. "But you kind of got used to it."

The comedian was skilled at making people feel uncomfortable. In his nightclub act, he would make believe that he was a recent immigrant to the United States who had a poor command of the English language. All his jokes would be delivered in a thick accent, and few of them would be funny. After awhile, the audience would start to giggle, thinking that Kaufman was a poor soul who did not belong on the stage. When this happened he would stop his act suddenly, accuse the audience of "laughing *at* me instead of *with* me," and pretend to be crying.

Sometimes he would intentionally try to bore his audience. Once, he came on stage, reading aloud from the book *The Great Gatsby*. After a few minutes, the audience began to stir. Kaufman acted very insulted. He shut the book, scolded the audience for interrupting him, and then continued to read. Another time, he ate dinner on stage, while the audience looked on in confusion.

On the set of *Taxi*, Kaufman claimed to be two people: Andy Kaufman and another character named Tony Clifton. Clifton "was a guy who he claimed was not him, but a friend of his," Glen says. "This was an obnoxious, chain-smoking guy who wore a lot of jewelry."

Kaufman demanded that his "friend" Tony Clifton be given a role on *Taxi*. Because the comedian insisted that Clifton was another person, he also asked for a separate contract, dressing room, and parking space. The producers played along at first, but eventually determined that Clifton's role was not right for the show. When Kaufman found out, he went into character as Tony Clifton. "If you're going to fire me, you better bring security guards," he threatened. "And I want to be fired on stage."

"We all went down and fired him on stage," Glen says with a chuckle. "He started yelling at us, 'You'll never work in this town again,' and all that. And the guards had to escort him out. Then, Andy Kaufman returned to the set of *Taxi* like everything was normal. Not a word was said about Tony Clifton."

When Kaufman died of cancer several years later, his associates wondered if he was not pulling another stunt. "There were a lot of people who thought that, when he died, it was a hoax," laughs Les. "Maybe it was. I'm still not sure."

Despite Kaufman's antics, *Taxi* was hailed as one of the most entertaining television programs ever. All together, the show ran for five years and was highly acclaimed by the critics. The Charles brothers won six Emmy Awards for their work on the program. Jim won two.

By this time, the three men all shared the same agent, who one day suggested that they combine their skills. The trio thought this was an excellent idea and formed a production company called Charles/Burrows/Charles. Once they were all set up, the three partners began throwing around ideas for new programs. The more they spoke, the more excited they became. In a very short time, these discussions would lead to the creation of a remarkable and unforgettable show that would go down in television history.

Woody signs for a package on a *Cheers* episode in which an orangutan
delivered the mail.

Making *Cheers*

"We figured the main set

would be a hotel bar.

Then we said 'If we have the bar,

do we need anything else?'"

—*Glen Charles*

The partners' agent stirred up interest at the NBC network in a program that would be created and produced by the three. The agent reminded the network of his clients' credentials: their Emmy Awards, senses of humor, and good-natured personalities. NBC, which was then the lowest-rated network in the United States, needed talented people to create new shows. With the agent's urging, the network agreed to air thirteen episodes of the partners' production.

Now, the pressure was on Glen, Les, and Jim to come up with something really good. The three wanted to do a program similar to *Taxi*, in which a group of characters, rather than a single actor or actress, would be the driving comedic force of the series.

"One thing we liked about *Taxi* was that it was a 'gang comedy,'" Glen says. "There really wasn't a star that the show revolved around. Everyone was a star."

The producers also wanted to make some changes. On *Taxi*, the characters driving cabs and hanging around the taxi garage wished they were someplace else, which sometimes created a dreary feeling.

"The one negative about *Taxi* was that the garage was a dark, gloomy place," Glen says. "It was a show about losers with big dreams."

The partners wanted their new show to take place in a more positive setting. All three were fans of *Fawlty Towers*, the British comedy starring Monty Python's John Cleese, which is set in an inn. They considered having their new program take place in a fancy hotel. Then they decided against it.

Because of the Charles brothers' background, they originally thought of setting the show just outside Las Vegas. Gamblers and other characters, in search of riches, would wander in and out, mingling with the regular cast.

"We figured the main set would be the hotel bar," Glen says. "Then, we said, 'If we have the bar, do we need anything else? We're not going to go up to the people's rooms. So why not just make it in a bar?'"

There are many types of bars in the United States: bars for cowboys, bars for motorcycle gangs, and singles' bars. The partners chose to place their show in a sports bar. The reasoning was simple: Glen loved hockey's Los Angeles Kings, and Jim was a fanatic fan of football's New York Giants and basketball's New York Knicks. Since sports were a big part of the producers' lives, they knew they would understand the thoughts of the sports fans that were being portrayed on the program.

After some talk, the three came up with the idea of having a sports bar owned by a former athlete. But the program would not be just about sports. There would also be romance.

"Back in those days, there wasn't romance on sitcoms (the television term for comedies; short for 'situation comedies') at all," Jim says. "So we thought we'd do something different—combine sports and romance."

Now, it was time for the partners to do some firsthand research. Writers who are creating a show about knights will often travel to Europe and tour castles. For a program about baseball, they might hang around stadiums and watch the players practice. If the production is about detectives, they go on calls with the local police department.

To research *Cheers*, Glen, Les, and Jim went from bar to bar, eavesdropping on conversations. They soon discovered that many people went to certain bars, not for the alcohol, but for the friendly atmosphere of companionship. This was the type of place they wanted the bar on their show to imitate.

Les particularly remembers one spot where, he says, every person knew each other by sight. "They weren't friends outside the bar," he explains, "but they were used to seeing each other in the bar. We were sitting there, listening to them have this extended conversation about canned soup. They were all really into it. One person would talk, then he'd stop, there'd be this long silence, and then the next person would start talking about cauliflower soup or something like that. They were having the time of their lives."

The lesson was that ridiculous conversations sometimes seem normal when everybody is having fun in a bar. Inspired by this experience, the writers created a discussion on the first episode of *Cheers* about the sweatiest movie ever made. Incidentally, this was a topic they had actually heard discussed during their tour of drinking establishments!

Because alcoholism is a serious problem in America, the producers were careful not to send out the message that getting drunk was the thing to do. "We were worried about the negative aspects of bars," Glen says. "We wanted to stay away from drunken humor." In fact, they wrote the character of bar owner Sam Malone—played by Ted Danson—as a recovering alcoholic to reinforce their ideas.

Glen, Jim, and Les together on the *Cheers* set during their first years with the series.

The partners took some time trying to figure out where the bar would be located. Eventually, they decided on the East Coast, where people tend to live in tight-knit ethnic neighborhoods and bars often serve as a type of community service and social center.

"At first, we thought about setting the show in New York," Glen says. "But there were so many shows already there." Looking for good locations, he visited Boston with his wife Mary Ann, "and just fell in love with the place."

While in Boston, the couple decided to continue their research by visiting a few taverns. Mary Ann opened the Yellow Pages and began looking for bars that sounded interesting. The Bull & Finch was near the top of the list, and it was within walking distance of the couple's hotel. As soon as they stepped through the door, Glen felt he had found the right spot. "I liked the sports bar feel," he says. "Everyone was very excited about the Boston sports teams. The whole atmosphere was very pleasant."

The one thing that bothered Glen was the fact that customers had to walk down a flight of stairs from the street level to enter the tavern. But he soon came to believe that this physical limitation lended a unique quality to the establishment. "I began to like the fact that the patrons could see a new customer entering by legs passing in the window," he says, "and stepping down into this world."

Of course, certain changes were made. The bar at the Bull & Finch is against one wall, while *Cheers* had a round bar in the center of the room—to accommodate better camera angles. Another change had to do with the Boston accent, which is very distinctive. Highly influenced by the waves of Irish immigrants who came to the city, the Boston way of speaking is like no other. Yet, when the partners were looking for a cast for *Cheers,* they had difficulty finding actors with believable Boston accents.

"We found it very tough to find people with Boston accents," Glen recalls. "The reason for that is every actor or actress who came from Boston went to speech class as soon as they left, so their accents wouldn't stand out. When they tried to do a Boston accent, after having it ripped out of them, it was a mess. It sounded more like people imitating a Boston accent."

As a result, some critics would later complain that none of the characters on *Cheers* (except mailman Cliff) had a Boston accent. The producers' response was that, regardless of the way the people spoke, the bar still *felt* just like a friendly tavern in that city.

In every bar, there is a customer like Norm Peterson, the character the Charles brothers created who constantly sits at the bar every night until it closes. It did not take a lot of thought to develop this idea. From his bartending days in Redlands, Les knew a man who fit this description perfectly.

"His name was Don, and he worked in a bank," Les says. "After work, he'd always come in for *one* beer—and end up staying until closing time. His wife would call, and he'd say, 'Tell her I just left. I'm on my way out.'"

George Wendt was the actor that was chosen for the role of Norm. Wendt is a jolly-looking man who spent two and a half years traveling through Europe and Africa with his college friends. While camping out in Algeria, Tunisia, and Morocco, he had entertained his companions by putting on his own comedy shows for them under the stars.

When he returned to his home town of Chicago, he decided to take lessons in the world-famous Second City comedy troupe. "I tried desperately to think of a profession I wouldn't hate," Wendt explains. His career choice paid off. Before being picked for *Cheers*,

Glen pauses in between takes with John Ratzenberger, who played Cliff Clavin, and George Wendt, who played Norm Peterson.

he guest-starred on *Taxi* and *M*A*S*H*, as well as such programs as *Soap* and *Alice*.

John Ratzenberger was another actor who auditioned for the part of Norm. Although he did not receive the role, he made a suggestion to the producers that got them thinking.

"Do you have anybody at the bar who's kind of a loud mouth?" he asked, "a guy who thinks he's the foremost authority of everything?"

Ratzenberger did not have as much acting experience as did many of the others trying out for *Cheers*, but he seemed to understand this character well. "He blew us all away," Jim recalls. "We all said, 'Oh God, we have to have this character in the show.'"

The actor walked out of the audition with a job—not playing Norm, as he had originally hoped, but rather a new character named Cliff Clavin. Cliff was a mailman who was convinced he was a genius. He bragged to everyone that he was the bar's trivia master—thanks to all the magazines he read while delivering mail.

Originally, Cliff was supposed to appear in just seven shows during the first year *Cheers* was on the air. But Ratzenberger was not about to let this opportunity end so quickly. By the time *Cheers* went off the air in 1993, he was still part of the weekly cast.

Rhea Perlman portrayed the hot-tempered barmaid, Carla Tortelli. The partners already knew Rhea from *Taxi*, where she occasionally appeared as the girlfriend of Louie, played by her real-life husband, Danny DeVito. She was a hard-working actress, who had appeared in many plays, theater groups, and short films. She was so dedicated to her craft that she would take any kind of job to support it. Once, she even allowed a doctor to test allergies on her in order to make money to fund her acting.

Shelley Long was working on her fourth movie, *Nightshift*, when she was asked to try out for the role of Diane Chambers, the intellectual barmaid at *Cheers*. Initially, she was hesitant to get involved with a television show. After all, she was well on her way to becoming a movie star. But the *Cheers* script impressed her.

"It was good," she says. "It was better than good. It was great. It was the best TV script I'd ever read. My movie career was beginning to pick up speed, so it seemed like a stupid time to commit…to a TV show. But this one seemed special. Real special."

Shelley had worked in Boston and was familiar with the type of people who hung around in the city's barrooms. In fact, she had visited the actual bar that Glen had in mind when he first started writing *Cheers*.

"I knew that bar and I knew Boston," she says. "I also knew Diane Chambers, or at least I knew women like her." Clearly, she liked this character, and the partners liked her. Shelley got the role.

Ted Danson was selected to play Diane's sometime boyfriend, Sam Malone, the owner of the bar. Danson was the son of an archaeologist whose good looks had won him a contract as the "Aramis Man" in ads for Aramis cologne. Ted had acted in every type of production, from performing Shakespeare in New York's Central Park to appearing on such soap operas as *The Doctors* and *Somerset.* In addition to his role as a police officer in the movie *The Onion Field*, he had been a guest on television programs like *Laverne & Shirley, Family,* and *Magnum P.I.*

Like Shelley, Ted was awed by the richness of the writing on *Cheers.* "You could almost do another series out of the stuff that was thrown away the first two seasons," he says.

The first episode of *Cheers* was broadcast in the fall of 1982. On that program, the viewers were introduced to Diane, who ended up in the bar after being dumped by her fiancé. Although *Cheers* was a comedy, the episode was written so that the audience felt sorry for Diane. They did not want her to disappear back onto the streets of Boston. They wanted her to stay in the bar with the rest of the gang. By the end of the show, they got their wish: Diane was offered a position as a waitress at the bar. To this day, Jim fondly remembers the pilot—or first program—as his favorite. "You cared," he says. And, soon, so did millions of viewers. An eleven-year love affair with the show had just begun.

Creative Company

"When you're starting out,

you think that if a joke doesn't work,

you're dead. So we just

lived and died with

every joke, every line, every scene."

—Les Charles

Soon after *Cheers* began, the three partners realized that they needed the cooperation of everybody—from the top executives at NBC to the people hammering together the sets—to make the show work.

"When you become a producer," Glen admits, "you are put in a position to make decisions on things about which you have absolutely no background—costumes and sets. So you pretty much rely on other people, like stylists and set designers."

Although the partners were certain they had a good show, the majority of Americans were still watching other programs. That meant that everyone associated with *Cheers* had to think about the people sitting at home, switching through the channels. If they happened upon *Cheers* by accident, there had to be something special about the show to snare them in.

"Every joke had to be good," Glen says. "We assumed that every week, there was one person or one family who was going to give us a shot and tune us in. If we did a bad show that was it. So we really tried to make sure every word was right."

Remembers Les, "When you're starting out, you think that if a joke doesn't work, you're dead. So we just lived and died with every joke, every line, every scene."

One week, Jim directed about five different final scenes, until everyone was pleased with the way the program ended. "I'm not sure the one we came up with was better than the first one," Glen says. "But it does indicate how concerned we were with the quality of the show."

Although the Charles brothers were the main writers for the show, over the years, fifty additional writers worked under them. One of them was David Lee, a fellow University of Redlands graduate whom the brothers hired after they met at a 1983 writer's conference. "Glen and Les are stunning human beings," says Lee, who went on to become co-creator/executive producer for the now top-rated program, *Frasier.* "They were kind and gracious and gave me a shot....They are high up there on my list."

Glen describes the process of writing as a "collaborative" effort—meaning that everyone has to work together: "You're in the room with the other writers, and there's a lot of give and take. Sometimes, you can be in a room with ten or twelve people, and everybody's coming up with jokes. And that can really be a lot of fun."

On some programs, staff members tend to get offended when others offer criticism. Writers do not like to be told how to write. Directors resent being given suggestions about directing. Actors are insulted when people come up with acting tips. On *Cheers*, though, everyone was invited to make comments. Jim notes that, even though he was not a writer, the Charles brothers liked hearing him evaluate their scripts.

"They would always listen to me, just like my father would listen to me," he says. "They would challenge me, I would challenge them, and they would challenge each other. When there was criticism, it was always to make the show better. It was never, 'I'm more important than you.'"

Even Jim's father was persuaded to help out. After Abe Burrows watched the program, he was asked for advice. The elderly man told his son that he thought the Sam character was not quite right. He needed to come across as less refined in order to be believable as a former jock.

The actors also had a say in the way they were portrayed. "On *Cheers*, everyone was there for the good of everyone else," Jim says. "All three of us encouraged the cast to speak up. If you didn't like a joke, we wanted to know why you thought it should be changed. We didn't want any of the cast members to look at us and say, '*They're* doing a good show.' We wanted everyone to be able to say '*We're* doing a good show.'"

In reality, that statement was true. Since there was no star at the center of the show, every actor and actress equally contributed to *Cheers'* outstanding reputation.

"*Cheers* had to have one of the best casts on television," Glen says. "When you consider that you had such a large cast, and you never had to hide anybody from the camera, that's really re-markable. On other shows I worked on, there were actors who had a harder time than others at getting a laugh. But that wasn't true with *Cheers*. Whichever actor you went to could get you the laughs you needed."

Everyone associated with the program during the first few seasons still talks about Nicholas Colasanto, an aging actor who played the role of Ernie "Coach" Pantusso. Because he was older than the others on the show, Nicholas frequently gave them advice. In return, they would forgive him for forgetting his lines.

"Nick had a horrible time remembering his lines," Les laughs. "He just didn't have a good memory. So he would have to write his lines down in various parts of the bar—on the furni-ture, wherever he was standing. If you go into the storage room today and find the old set from *Cheers*, you can still see Nick's handwriting on walls and chairs."

"Cheers had to have one of the best casts on television."

But the two actors mainly responsible for drawing early viewers to the show were Ted Danson and Shelley Long. As Sam and Diane, the romantic tension between them added sparks to the program—and kept people tuning in to find out what would happen next.

"Ted and Shelley were great," Jim says. "Everyone loved Sam. Half the people loved Diane. And the other half wanted to grab her and shake her. Either way, they were interested."

The adventures of Sam and Diane went through many twists and turns. During the second season of the program, Diane left the bar to work at an art gallery. There, actor Christopher Lloyd played a wacky artist who tried to convince her to dump the *Cheers* owner. The next year, the couple split up. Diane started dating Dr. Frasier Crane—played by actor Kelsey Grammer. Frasier proposed to Diane, and the two flew to Europe to marry. Sam followed them to try to stop the wedding, but he could not locate the couple. Viewers had to wait until the next season to learn the outcome. Sam eventually tracked his love to a convent, where she was working after breaking up with Frasier.

Glen's favorite episode was "Diane's Perfect Date." Sam and Diane were not romantically involved at the time, and each had decided to set the other up with a dream date. Sam was certain that Diane was going to present herself as his date. When she showed up accompanied by another woman, the bar owner had to quickly find a partner for Diane. He rushed into the pool room and picked out a stranger—who turned out to be a murderer.

"People got very caught up in the relationship," Les says. "When things didn't go a certain way, we'd get these really angry letters. People would say, 'For God's sake, I hear you're thinking about breaking them up. I'll never watch the show again if you break them up.' All the cast would get letters addressed to them as their characters. Some people thought the characters were real, which is scary."

In case certain viewers were not aware of the latest developments in the characters' lives, the

Jim helped to keep *Cheers* going for eleven years by using his great talents from behind the camera.

writers would do their best to update the public every week.

Explains Jim, "You can't assume that everyone's been watching your show from the beginning. For a television show to grow in popularity, people have to tell people. It's not like a movie, where people rush out and see it because they're afraid that it's going to leave the theater. People wait for others to tell them, 'You should really check this show out.'

"Glen and Les were very shrewd. They taught me that on every show, you had to tell the new viewers who the characters were. You had to say, 'Diane's a terrible waitress, but she's working here because she likes Sam. Sam likes Diane. Carla hates Diane. Norm loves beer. Cliff thinks he knows everything.'"

It took a long time for *Cheers* to draw new viewers. After the first season, it was all the way down in seventy-first place of all programs broadcast on national networks.

"The first two years, we had very poor ratings," Glen recalls. "It was very discouraging. We were dead last a couple of weeks, and that was depressing. We knew we were getting laughs from the studio audience. And after the first year, we won an Emmy for best show. So we knew we were doing something good. We just needed people to discover us.

"The bottom line was we knew this was a show we'd never be embarrassed about. It might not be a success. It might have bad ratings. But we liked the show, and the people who saw it liked it, too."

Sometimes people found out about *Cheers* during the summer, when reruns were broadcast. "Then, the gardener or the pool man would tell me, 'I saw your show. It was pretty good,'" Jim explains. "And I had to believe them. I figured if they didn't like the show, they wouldn't bother saying anything."

Strangely, the bad ratings built a stronger bond between the partners. "It drew us together," Les says. "We consoled each other, picked each other up. It was us against the world. In some ways, the bad times are more important than the good times. Some people might turn on each other when things are bad. We only became closer."

After hoping that their luck would turn around, the producers finally got their wish. NBC placed the incredibly popular *Cosby Show*, starring comedian Bill Cosby, in a slot before *Cheers*. After *Cosby* ended, many viewers did not bother changing the channel. Slowly, America began to go wild over *Cheers*.

"For the rest of our lives, Bill Cosby will always have a warm place in our hearts," Les jokes with a chuckle.

By 1985, *Cheers* was a nationwide sensation. It was one of the top ten shows in the country and earned $115 million in advertising fees for

"For the rest of our lives, Bill Cosby will always have a warm place in our hearts."

NBC. By following their hearts, the partners had gotten the success they had always wanted.

"Everything worked for us," Jim says. "We came around at the right time. We had the right casting. And we were on the right network. NBC was in last place. They had nothing to replace us with."

Highs and Lows

"*Cheers* was not just about one person."

—*Glen Charles*

During the third year of *Cheers*, the show suffered a terrible tragedy. Nicholas Colasanto, the actor who played Coach, died. The cast was so upset that they had to take a break from their filming schedule.

Colasanto had been ill for some time, and his heart condition kept worsening. "He was getting older and weaker," Les says. "And it takes a lot of stamina to do a show. Sometimes, he'd be hospitalized, and we had to write him out of the episodes."

Yet, Nick always had managed to return to the set, and the people at *Cheers* expected him to be around as long as the show was on the air. When news of his death reached the cast, they were crushed.

"The death was very devastating to us all," says Jim. "Nick was a father figure to everyone on the show, including me. We all knew he was

sick. But when he died, we had to shut down.
We just couldn't do the show."

The remaining scripts of the season had to be
rewritten, without Coach. The producers had to
find someone to replace him. Another older man
would not work; there was only one Coach.

Instead, the partners decided to introduce a
young man to the *Cheers* audience. Actor Woody
Harrelson had appeared in the Broadway play
Biloxi Blues, and had co-starred in the movie
Wildcats with Goldie Hawn. On *Cheers*, he
played Woody Boyd, an Indiana farm boy whose
dream is to work as a bartender in the big city.

According to the plot, Woody had been ex-
changing letters with Coach and finally had
come to Boston to visit him. When he arrived
at the bar, Sam had to tell him the bad news:
Coach had passed away. However, Sam needed
help behind the bar, and Woody was perfect for
the job.

The third season may have been the toughest
for the partners. Besides Nick's death, they had
to deal with two pregnancies—those of Shelley
Long and Rhea Perlman. Rhea's condition was
worked into the program—Carla was supposed
to be carrying her sixth child. But the decision
was made to ignore Shelley's pregnancy. As a result, the actress frequently performed in scenes
with her stomach hidden behind the bar.

"We talked about a way of making Shelley's
pregnancy part of the story," Les says. "We just

"… The bar
became the
star of the
show."

couldn't find a situation everyone was happy with. So we tried to hide it, and I think we did a horrible job. I still think we could have used her pregnancy—it would have made the show more of a soap opera. But we couldn't find a way that everyone would have liked—me, Glen, Jim, Shelley, and the network."

At the end of the fifth season, the producers were faced with an even bigger problem: Shelley Long made the decision to leave the program to pursue her movie career.

"Several critics said it would be the end of *Cheers*," Glen says. "We felt, 'Well, we're not going to fold our tents. We still have an audience. We're still a highly rated show.' *Cheers* was not just about one person."

Jim believes that, for the first five seasons, Sam and Diane's romance was the focus of *Cheers*. "After Shelley left," he says, "the bar became the star of the show."

The partners were still faced with replacing the actress. "The one thing we decided was we weren't going to come up with another Shelley," Les says. Rather than a sweet-faced blonde, the producers hired the brown-haired, more conservative-seeming Kirstie Alley.

Kirstie, a native of Wichita, Kansas, moved to Los Angeles to become an actress. Instead of finding fame, she ended up decorating houses. Then, after five years in California, her fortunes changed. She won a role in *Star Trek II: The*

Jim discusses an upcoming episode in the dressing room with the *Cheers* cast while they get into costume.

Wrath of Khan. Her character on *Cheers*, Rebecca Howe, took over the bar while Sam was traveling around the world, trying to get over his breakup with Diane. When Sam returned to *Cheers*, he found himself working for the newcomer—and eventually dating her.

Glen had seen Kirstie act before and was not sure of the range of her talents. "I didn't think she was that funny," he says. "But she was glamorous and a good actress. I felt she'd bring out the funny qualities in other people. But she had comedic qualities we weren't aware of. She turned out to be one of the funniest people I've ever seen. She can do a very funny joke—she can even cry funny. She was supposed to be an authority figure everyone was at odds with. But people liked her because, when she was confronted, she just turned into jello."

Another addition to the *Cheers* cast was the actress Bebe Neuwirth, who played Dr. Lilith Sternim. Bebe had been interested in performing since age five, when she started taking ballet lessons. Before *Cheers*, she had appeared on Broadway in *Sweet Charity*—(for which she won a prized Tony Award), *A Chorus Line, Dancin',* and other plays. As a cast member on *Cheers*, she portrayed a straight-laced psychiatrist who was dating Frasier. Over time, she ended up marrying him.

"We introduced Bebe during the fourth season, when we wanted to show Frasier on the worst date he ever had," Les says. "But she was so good that, by the seventh season, she was a regular."

From time to time, Frances Sternhagen appeared on the show, amusing audiences in her role as Esther Clavin, Cliff's mother. During the fifth season, she drove Cliff crazy by moving in with Woody. Another time, she became so taken with her son's girlfriend that she nearly forced him to marry her. In another episode, she accompanied Cliff to his appearance on NBC's *Tonight Show*—and embarrassed him by joining host Johnny Carson on stage.

As the years went on, *Cheers* became a magical experience for Jim. Just as his childhood was spent at his father's rehearsals, he now happily watched his daughters—Katherine, Elizabeth, and Margaret—on the set.

"They liked to come to work with me and run around the stage, like I used to do as a kid," he says. "I have so many fond memories of that. I remember sitting on (actress) Virginia Martin's lap. And, then, my kids would come to the set of *Cheers* and sit on Kirstie's lap.

"I don't necessarily want my daughters to go into the business. But if they go into show business like I went into show business, it would be okay."

As the years went on, Cheers became a magical experience for Jim.

Chapter 8

Closing Up

"We talked about ending

the show for a number of years. . .

When we did, it was great

to go out on top."

—*Jim Burrows*

As *Cheers* continued to soar in popularity, movie producers approached the show's stars to appear in films. Since most Americans already recognized these faces, it made sense to put them on movie posters. While *Cheers* was achieving top ratings, Kirstie Alley was featured in *Look Who's Talking* and *Mad House*; Woody Harrelson co-starred in *Doc Hollywood, White Men Can't Jump,* and *Indecent Proposal*; and Ted Danson stood out in *Three Men and a Baby, Dad, Made in America,* and other productions.

The partners were also busy with new projects. At one point, they tried to follow in the tradition of Mary Tyler Moore's production company, starting what television professionals call a "comedy factory." That is a production company that does several hit comedies at the same time.

The threesome came up with two programs, *All Is Forgiven* and *The Tortellis. All Is Forgiven* took place behind the scenes at a soap opera. *The Tortellis* was a *Cheers* "spin-off"—the term for a show based on characters who first appeared on another program. Through the years, there have been many successful spin-offs. In the 1960s, *Gomer Pyle* emerged from *The Andy Griffith Show.* During the next decade, *Happy Days* spun off both *Laverne & Shirley* and *Mork & Mindy.* Today, the enormously popular *Frasier* is based on that character from the *Cheers* cast.

The Tortellis was supposed to be about a disgusting couple, based on Carla's ex-husband, Nick Tortelli—played by Dan Hedaya—and his pretty but dumb wife, Loretta—played by Jean Kasem. NBC wanted *The Tortellis* to be the opposite of the wholesome family on Bill Cosby's program.

Neither *The Tortellis* nor *All Is Forgiven* gained nationwide interest. The partners largely blame themselves for this failure. Their hearts were simply too much involved with *Cheers* to give adequate effort to anything else.

"We were taking on too much," Jim explains. "It was hard to split our time. I'd say the lesson of this is, instead of dividing yourself all over the place, do *one* great show."

However, the producers had started wondering how long *Cheers* could last. "By the ninth or tenth year, we were feeling that the stories were

"By the ninth or tenth year, we were feeling that the stories were just a little harder to come by."

just a little harder to come by," Glen admits.

"Every time someone would come up with a
story, we'd say, 'Don't you remember? We did
something like that during our third season.' It
seemed like we'd pretty much told the story of
every character. Without adding another character, we felt like we were spinning our wheels."

That did not mean that there were no great
moments still to come. During the last season,
there was a hilarious episode in which Cliff was
convinced that his next-door neighbor was Adolf
Hitler. Frasier's wife, Lilith, left him, causing
him to threaten to kill himself by jumping off a
window ledge. When she decided to return to
her husband, she was shocked to discover that
he was in bed with Rebecca!

But the partners did choose to end *Cheers*
when Ted Danson announced that he would not
return after the eleventh season.

"We talked about ending the show for a
number of years," Jim says. "When Ted decided
to leave, we talked about possibly doing a show
without the character of Sam Malone. That conversation lasted less than a minute—Sam was so
much a part of the show. We would not have
ended *Cheers* if Ted had chosen not to leave. But
when we did, it was great to go out on top."

Unlike so many other television programs,
which remain on the air for several years after
their popularity has faded, *Cheers* was still in the
top ten by the time the last episode aired.

Americans loved the show and would remember it fondly after it finished.

"People were still watching," Glen says. "We didn't overstay our welcome."

The partners wanted to make the program's final season an interesting one so they came up with a series of situations that actually mirrored real life. It all began when Rebecca accidentally started a fire that burned down most of the bar. *Cheers* was reconstructed, but the times had changed. A new saloon had opened up nearby,

Jim, Glen, and Les put some finishing touches on a script during one of the final seasons of *Cheers*.

complete with high-tech video games and dancing girls. Like Americans everywhere who are today abandoning well-established local businesses for giant "superstores," *Cheers'* customers now preferred the modern bar.

The final episode of *Cheers*—the last of 275 shows—aired on May 20, 1993. Although Glen and Les had largely passed on the writing responsibilities to others by this time, they decided to write this segment together. As a special surprise, Shelley Long made a return appearance as Diane Chambers—after a six-year absence—and immediately restarted her romance with old flame, Sam Malone.

When the show ended that night, NBC broadcast a half-hour special called *Last Call: A Cheers Celebration*, which was a tribute to a program that had charmed and humored the American public for more than a decade. The cast members were now huge celebrities and had endless choices about the types of projects they could do. Still, they were just as sad as the program's fans to see *Cheers* leave the airwaves.

"I feel really fortunate that I spent six years of my life having an experience that most people will never see in a lifetime," Kirstie Alley said at the time. "All my memories are good memories—and I'll always have that, forever. So even if I'm sad for a little while that it's over, the good far outweighs the bad."

"All my memories are good memories," Kirstie Alley said.

"No one could
wish for better
partners," Jim
has said.

🍎🍎🍎🍎🍎

As for the partners, they were overwhelmed by how popular their show had become. "The success still bewilders us," Les says. "I still don't understand it." But Jim has his own theory. The many merits of the partnership, he insists, turned *Cheers* into extraordinary entertainment.

"No one could wish for better partners," he says. "It was not only a partnership of creative ability, but a partnership of love and mutual respect. There was no back-stabbing. Everything was out in the open. And I think the quality of the show was a reflection of the quality of the partnership."

Moving Ahead

"When three people

can get along under

[these] circumstances,

you really can't ask for more.

I really feel blessed

by this partnership."

—*Les Charles*

Of the three partners, James Burrows remains most visible. With nine Emmy Awards to his credit, he is one of the most sought-after directors in Hollywood. As someone who grew up in the theater, he has a hard time staying away from the business of entertainment.

Throughout his career, Jim has kept himself busy with numerous projects, directing television shows like *Night Court* and *Dear John*; the TV movie *More Than Friends*, starring Rob Reiner and Penny Marshall; and the film *Partners*, with actors Ryan O'Neal and John Hurt.

"Jim understands acting, which a lot of directors don't," says actor John Larroquette, who worked with Burrows on *Night Court*. "He's excellent at inspiring you to do what you do best. He understands comedy better than many actors."

After *Cheers*, Jim chose to divide his time directing two NBC comedies, *Friends* and *Frasier*, which was created to center around the character of Dr. Frasier Crane.

"It was natural for me to do *Frasier*," he says, pointing out his long-time relationship with the program's star, Kelsey Grammer. "I love Kelsey, and it's great to see him jump from being a supporting actor to the leading actor."

Although the Charles brothers are not involved in *Frasier*, both are happy to see their friend Kelsey getting the recognition they feel he deserves. "I think he might be the best actor I ever worked with," Les says. "People used to be surprised when we said that. Now that he's gone out on his own, they understand."

The brothers have also continued writing scripts together. One film they hope to make is a romantic comedy that revolves around a man who pretends to be a hero Navy pilot in order to impress his fiancé's dying father.

The Charles brothers both look forward to the day they will once again work with Jim. "We'd love to work on another television project with him, and hope we will," says Glen.

As of now, the three have only teamed up on one program after *Cheers*: a comedy about an aging actress living in Hollywood in the late 1930s who is still dreaming of her glory days. One episode of the show ran, but the audience showed little interest.

"We thought this was something that could inspire us after *Cheers*," Jim says. "But it just didn't work. We don't know why. We're still trying to figure that out."

With all their success, though, bad reviews no longer discourage the partners. Every time they have been down before, they have bounced back stronger than ever. No doubt they will meet again in the future and exchange jokes and ideas until they create another hit.

In the meantime, fans everywhere are wondering whether the *Cheers* cast will get together another time for a special reunion show. In 1994, Les said, "It's a little early. I think we should wait a little while until people really miss us. Then, I'm sure it will happen."

No matter what the future holds, each partner feels enriched by the past. Their skill at developing classic television—and lifelong friendships—has left all three feeling happily fulfilled.

"It's hard enough to have a partnership if you're running a hardware store," Les says. "It's another thing when you're trying to be creative.

It's tough for a writer to be criticized, to be told, 'That doesn't work.' You put your heart and guts into your work and take it so personally. When three people can get along under those circumstances, you really can't ask for more. I really feel blessed by this partnership."

Appendix: Highlights from Eleven Years of *Cheers*

Season 1: 1982–1983
• After being dumped by her fiancé, Diane Chambers is offered a waitressing job at *Cheers*.
• Boston Congressman Tip O'Neill—Speaker of the House at the time—visits the bar.
• Sam and Coach both try to date the same woman; she picks Coach.

Season 2: 1983–1984
• Sam and Diane begin dating.
• Cliff wants to marry Carla's twin sister, Annette.
• Carla delivers her fifth child.
• Diane temporarily leaves the bar to work in an art gallery.
• A crazy artist tries to convince Diane to leave Sam.
• A customer wills $100,000 to *Cheers*.
• Sam tells Diane, "I love you."

Season 3: 1984-1985
• Diane starts dating Frasier.
• Coach becomes engaged, but his fiancée breaks up with him after winning the lottery.
• Frasier's mother threatens to kill Diane.
• Carla becomes pregnant with her sixth child.
• Diane becomes "allergic" to Frasier.

- Frasier and Diane plan to marry in Europe.
- Sam flies to Europe to stop the wedding but cannot find the couple.

Season 4:   1985–1986
- Diane breaks up with Frasier before getting married, and Sam finds her working in a convent.
- Sam and Diane nearly get back together when their plane is about to crash.
- Woody comes to *Cheers* looking for Coach and learns he has passed away. Sam offers the young man a job bartending.
- Senator Gary Hart visits the bar.
- Sam proposes to a mystery woman, but no one will know who she is until the next season.

Season 5:   1986–1987
- The mystery woman turns out to be Diane, but the wedding does not take place. Soon, the two are dating others.
- Frasier moves in with Lilith.
- Sam and Diane again plan to get married. The two buy a house, but a marriage counselor tries to talk them out of the wedding.
- Diane calls off the wedding. She moves to Maine to write a novel.

Season 6:   1987–1988
- Sam sells the bar and travels around the world, then returns to work for Rebecca.
- Sam tries to become a TV sportscaster.
- Frasier proposes to Lilith.
- Carla becomes pregnant with twins and marries Eddie Lebec.

- Woody becomes friends with actor Robert Urich—but no one believes him.
- Carla finds out she is going to be a grandmother.
- Baseball star Wade Boggs—then on the Boston Red Sox—visits the bar, but everyone thinks he is an impostor.

Season 7: 1989–1989
- Rebecca is temporarily fired, and Sam is promoted to bar manager.
- Woody begins dating well-to-do Kelly Gaines.
- Lilith learns she is pregnant.

Season 8: 1989–1990
- Sam and Rebecca share their first kiss.
- Rebecca starts dating a millionaire named Robin.
- Boston Mayor Raymond Flynn visits the bar.
- Lilith gives birth in a taxi cab; she and Frasier name the boy Frederick.
- Cliff competes on the game show *Jeopardy!*
- Robin is arrested for illegal stock-market activities.
- Robin catches Sam and Rebecca in a romantic moment.
- Sam buys back the bar.

Season 9: 1990–1991
- Under Sam, Rebecca again manages the bar.
- Robin returns to Rebecca; she visits him in prison.

- Cliff's mother moves in with Woody.
- Woody stars in a TV commercial.
- Rebecca agrees to marry Robin, then backs out at the last moment when she decides that she does not love him.
- Sam says he wants to become a father.

Season 10:   1991–1992

- Sam and Rebecca decide to have a baby together.
- A psychic tells Carla she has spiritual powers.
- Sam and Rebecca choose not to have a baby after all because they realize they are not in love.
- Harry Connick, Jr. plays Woody's cousin, who develops a crush on Rebecca.
- Sam joins a professional baseball team to prove he still has "what it takes."
- Cliff appears on *The Tonight Show* with Johnny Carson.
- Woody and Kelly marry.

Season 11:   1992–1993

- Norm finds a job as a beer taster.
- Lilith leaves Frasier, and he threatens to kill himself by jumping off a window ledge.
- Cliff is convinced that Adolph Hitler is his next-door neighbor.
- Rebecca accidentally starts a fire, and most of the bar burns down.
- Sam rebuilds the bar, but loses his customers to a more modern competitor.

Glossary

collaboration The act of working together on a project.

comedy factory A company producing several television comedies at the same time.

Emmy Award Television's highest honor.

on spec Taken from the term "on speculation," the process of randomly sending out scripts to studios. The writers hope—or "speculate"—that the studios will like their work.

pilot First episode of a television program. Often, before a TV series is launched, a pilot is shown. If viewers like the pilot, the series follows.

rewrite Fixing a script with problems: writing in new scenes, taking out bad ones, changing dialogue.

sitcom The television term for a comedy series; short for "situation comedy."

spin-off A program based on characters who first appeared on another show. For example, Kelsey Grammer first played Dr. Frasier Crane on *Cheers*. Later, Grammer would get his own show, *Frasier*, based on the same character.

Top Ten One of the Top Ten watched shows in the United States.

Further Reading

Blumenthal, Howard J. *Careers in Television*. New York: Little, Brown & Company, 1992.

Calabro, Marian. *Zap! A Brief History of Television*. New York: Macmillan, 1992.

Cheney, Glenn A. *Television in American Society*. New York: Watts, 1983.

Cruise, Beth. *Behind the Scenes at "Saved by the Bell": An Inside Look at TV's Hottest Teen Show*. New York: Macmillan, 1992.

Shachtman, Tom, and Shelare, Harriet. *Video Power: A Complete Guide to Writing, Planning, and Shooting Videos*. New York: Henry Holt, 1988.

Television. Troy, MI: International Book Center, 1987.

Bibliography

Fenten, Don, and Fenten, Barbara. *Behind the Television Scene*. Mankato, MN: Crestwood House, 1980.

Wenger, Mark. *The Cheers Trivia Book*. New York: Citadel Press, 1994.

Lovece, Frank and Franco, Jules. *Hailing Taxi*. New York: Prentice Hall, 1988.

Chronology

December 30, 1940 James "Jim" Burrows is born in Los Angeles, California.

February 18, 1943 Glen Charles is born outside of Las Vegas, Nevada.

1945 James Burrows moves to New York, where his father, Abe Burrows—introduces him to television and the Broadway stage.

March 25, 1948 Les Charles is born outside of Las Vegas, Nevada.

1965 After completing Music and Art High School in New York City and Oberlin College in Ohio, Jim graduates from the Yale School of Drama.

—He soon meets actress Mary Tyler Moore while working backstage on her play Breakfast at Tiffany's. Within a few years, she will have her own top-rated television show—and Jim will wind up directing numerous episodes.

1968 After completing Basic High School in Las Vegas and the University of Redlands in California—and attending law school at the University of California at Berkeley—Glen receives a master's degree in language arts from San Francisco State University.

1971 After completing Basic High School, Les graduates from the University of Redlands.

1974 Unhappy with their careers, Glen and Les try to become television writers. They send out scripts to all their favorite shows, and—after several months—receive a call from the program, M*A*S*H. Their first episode airs in 1975.

—Jim gets a job at MTM Productions, producers of the Mary Tyler Moore Show, Phyllis, and other programs.

1975 Jim meets the Charles brothers on the set of Phyllis; he's a director, they're writers.

1978 Jim and the Charles brothers go their separate ways until meeting again on the show *Taxi*. For the next five years, they work together regularly. Les and Glen will win six Emmy Awards—television's highest honor—for their contributions to the program. Jim will win two. By the time *Taxi* ends, the three decide to start their own production company, called Charles/Burrows/Charles.

Fall 1982 After forming their new partnership, the three create the first episode of *Cheers*, a comedy about a friendly bar in Boston.

1983 For the first two seasons, *Cheers* draws poor ratings. The partners—convinced they have a good show—keep trying hard, waiting for the country to discover the program.

1984-1985 The *Cheers* cast is shaken by the death of Nicholas Colasanto, who played the character known as Coach. He will be replaced by Woody Harrelson.
—Actresses Shelley Long and Rhea Perlman become pregnant. The producers try to disguise Shelley's condition by placing her behind the bar during certain scenes.

1985 *Cheers* is a huge success, one of America's Top Ten programs.

1987 Shelley Long leaves *Cheers* to continue her movie career. She will be replaced by Kirstie Alley.

1993 *Cheers* star Ted Danson announces that he will leave the program after its eleventh season. The partners decide to end the show, rather than produce *Cheers* without him.

May 20, 1993 Millions of viewers across America watch the final episode of *Cheers*, the last of 275 memorable programs.

1994 James Burrows directs the two programs, *Friends* and the enormously popular *Frasier*, featuring *Cheers* star Kelsey Grammer. The Charles brothers work on a new script together—tailored for the movies instead of TV. The three partners look forward to working together again on a new project.

Index

🍎🍎🍎🍎🍎🍎🍎

Abe Burrows Show, 28
Alice, 70
Alley, Kirstie, 86–88, 91, 95. *See also*
  Cheers
All in the Family, 24
All Is Forgiven, 92
Awards, 9, 59, 80, 96

Ball, Lucille, 32–33
Betty White Show, 44
Bob Newhart Show, 54–55
Boston, as site for *Cheers,* 66–68
Boyd, Woody, 60, 85. *See also Cheers*
Bull & Finch, 67. *See also Cheers*
Burrows, Abe, 28–31, 34, 76
Burrows, Elizabeth, 89
Burrows, Jim. *See also* Charles, Burrows,
  and Charles
    aversion to show business, 33
    birth, 29
    childhood, 30–32
    children, 89
    Emmy Awards, 5, 59, 80, 96
    entertainment background, 9,
      28–31
    father's influence in directing, 37
    film work, 98
    first jobs, 36–38
    interest in directing, 36–37
    interest in singing, 33–34
    meets Charles brothers, 46, 48–49
    openness to others' ideas, 36–38,
      48
    parents, 28–31
    post-*Cheers* work, 98–99, 100
    schooling, 33–36
    seeing TV shows as mini–plays, 9,
      47
    TV influences, 32–33
    work on *Phyllis,* 46, 48–49
    work with Mary Tyler Moore and
      Grant Tinker, 46–47
Burrows, Katherine, 89
Burrows, Margaret, 89
Burrows, Ruth, 29

California, University of, 22
Car 54, Where Are You?, 32
Chambers, Diane, 71, 78, 85–86, 95.
  See also Cheers
Charles/Burrows/Charles production
  company, 59
Charles, Burrows, and Charles. *See also*
  specific partner
    differences between, 9–10
    Emmy Awards, 5, 59, 80
    first work together, 46, 49
    forming production company, 59
    getting TV advice, 51
    sharing credit, 11
    similarities between, 48–49
    working relationship, 96
    work on *Bob Newhart Show,*
      54–55
    work on *Cheers. See Cheers*
    work on *Phyllis,* 48–49, 54–55
    work on *Taxi,* 55–59. *See also*
      Taxi
Charles, Evelyn, 14–15, 20
Charles, Gerald, 14–15, 20
Charles, Les and Glen. *See also* Charles,
  Burrows, and Charles
    birth and childhood, 14–20
    decision to become writers,
      24–25
    early entertainment influences,
      18–19, 20, 24
    Emmy Awards, 5, 59, 80
    encouraging each other, 25
    film work, 98
    first TV writing attempts, 40–42
    meet Burrows, 46, 48–49
    Mormon influence on, 16
    non-TV jobs, 23–24
    parents, 14–15, 20
    post-*Cheers* work, 99–100
    as rewriters, 45
    schooling, 21–22
    work on *M*A*S*H,* 42–43
    work on *Mary Tyler Moore Show,*
      44

110

Charles, Mary Ann, 67
Charles, Zora, 23, 42
Cheers
    bar as star of, 86
    bar based on, 67
    becomes nationwide hit, 81–82
    cast
        assembling, 68–72
        Carla, 70–71, 85
        Cliff, 68, 69, 70
        Cliff's mom, 88
        Coach, 77, 84–85
        Diane, 71, 78, 85–86, 95
        Frasier, 78
        Lilith, 88
        movie work before *Cheers*,
          71–72, 85
        movie work since *Cheers*, 91
        Nick, 92
        Norm, 23, 68–70
        Rebecca, 87–88
        Sam, 65, 72, 78, 95
        Woody, 60, 85
    collaborative effort on, 76–77
    decision to end, 93
    developing idea for, 63–64
    final episode, 95
    final season, 94–95
    goes on air, 72
    inspiring real *Cheers* bars, 9
    partners begin tiring of, 92–93
    popularity of, 8–9, 79
    research for, 64–67
    reunion of, 100
    spin-offs, 92, 99
    writing for, 74–76
Clavin, Cliff, 68, 69, 70. *See also Cheers*
Clavin, Esther, 88. *See also Cheers*
Cleese, John, 63
"Clifton, Tony," 58–59
Colasanto, Nicholas, 77, 84–85
Cosby Show, 81
Crane, Frasier, 78. *See also Cheers*
Crane, Lilith Sternim, 88. *See also*
    Cheers

Dad, 91
Danson, Ted, 65, 72, 91, 93. *See also*
    Cheers
Danza, Tony, 56
Dear John, 98
DeVito, Danny, 56, 71

Dick Van Dyke Show, 18–19
Doc Hollywood, 91
Doctors, The, 72

Emmy Awards, 9, 59, 80, 96

Family, 72
Fawlty Towers, 63
Frasier, 99
Friends, 98–99

Gleason, Jackie, 18
Grammer, Kelsey, 78, 99
Gravas, Latka, 57
Green, Shecky, 20

Harrelson, Woody, 85, 91. *See also*
    Cheers
Hedeya, Dan, 92. *See also Cheers*
Henner, Marilu, 56
Hill Street Blues, 44
Hirsch, Judd, 56
Honeymooners, The, 18
Howe, Rebecca, 87–88. *See also Cheers*

I Love Lucy, 32
Indecent Proposal, 91

Kasem, Jean, 92
Kaufman, Andy, 57–59

Last Call: A Cheers Celebration, 95
Laverne & Shirley, 72
Leachman, Chloris, 45
Lee, David, 75
Lloyd, Christopher, 56, 78
Long, Shelley, 71, 78, 85–86. *See also*
    Cheers
Look Who's Talking, 91

*M*A*S*H*, 24, 42–43, 70
Made in America, 91
Mad House, 91
Magnum P.I., 72
Malone, Sam, 65, 72, 78, 95. *See also*
    Cheers
Mary Tyler Moore Show, 41, 44, 47
Moore, Mary Tyler, 18, 44, 46
More Than Friends, 98
Movies
    Burrows' work on, 98
    Cheers cast members in, 71–72,
      85, 91

Charles brothers' work on, 98
MTM, 44

Neuwirth, Bebe, 88. *See also Cheers*
Nevada, University of, 22
Night Court, 98

Oberlin College, 35
Onion Field, The, 72

Pantuso, Ernie, 77, 84–85. *See also Cheers*
Partners, 98
Perlman, Rhea, 70–71, 85. *See also Cheers*
Peterson, Norm, 23, 68–70. *See also Cheers*
Phyllis
    Charles brothers' work on, 45–46, 48–49, 54
    Charles, Burrows, and Charles' work on, 46, 48–49
    as MTM show, 44
PM East, PM West, 31

Ratzenberger, John, 69, 70. *See also Cheers*
Rhoda, 44
Rickles, Don, 20

Second City comedy troupe, 69
Silvers, Phil, 32
Sitcoms (situation comedies), 64

60 Minutes, 31
Soap, 70
Somerset, 72
Spin-offs, 92
Star Trek II: The Wrath of Khan, 86–87
Sternhagen, Frances, 88. *See also Cheers*
Sternim, Lilith, 88. *See also Cheers*

Taxi
    cast of, 56–59
    Charles, Burrows, and Charles work on, 55–59
    Cheers actors appearing on, 70, 71
Three Men and a Baby, 91
Tinker, Grant, 44, 46
Tony Randall Show, 44
Tortelli, Carla, 70–71, 85. *See also Cheers*
Tortelli, Nick, 92
Tortellis, The, 92

University of California at Berkeley, 22
University of Nevada, 22
University of Redlands, 21-22
University of San Francisco, 22

Van Dyke, Dick, 18–19

Wendt, George, 68–70. *See also Cheers*
White Men Can't Jump, 91
Wildcats, 85

Yale School of Drama, 35
You'll Never Get Rich, 32

Photo Credits

Cover and cover inset: courtesy Paramount Pictures.
Photos on pages 6, 10, 12, 26, 60, 66, 69, 79, 87, 94, 101, 103, 104 and 105: courtesy Paramount Pictures.
Photos on pages 30 and 34 provided by James Burrows.
Photos on pages 20 and 55 provided by Glen and Les Charles.

Special thanks to Larry McCallister at Paramount for his valuable help in securing permission to reproduce many of the photos in this book.